The Heart of the Matter

A Compassionate Approach to Transforming Behaviors in Foster and Adopted Children

MEGAN M. HAMM, LPC, RPT

The Heart of the Matter: A Compassionate Approach to Transforming Behaviors in Foster and Adopted Children

Copyright © 2024 Megan M. Hamm, LLC

All rights reserved.

No part of this book may be reproduced, distributed, or transmitted in any form by any means, graphic, electronic, or mechanical, including photocopy, recording, taping, or by any information storage or retrieval system, without permission in writing from the publisher, except in the case of reprints in the context of reviews, quotes, or references.

Printed in the United States of America

Paperback ISBN: 979-8-9903090-0-5

E-book ISBN: 979-8-9903090-1-2

Dedicated to my family for always supporting me and putting up with the tireless nights of writing and tireless days of talking about this book.

Contents

Introduction ... 1
   Meet Cassie and Isabelle ... 9

Chapter 1 — The Heart of Meltdown Moments ... 11
   Moment of Truth ... 17

Chapter 2 — The Brain and Heart Connection ... 19
   Trauma and the Catch-All Closet ... 26
   Moment of Truth ... 30
   Parenting R + R ... 31
   Relationship with Self ... 32
   Relationship with Child ... 33

Chapter 3 — The Heart of Parenting ... 35
   Moment of Truth ... 39
   Stepping Outside the Book ... 40

Chapter 4 — Healing the Heart from Expectation ... 43
   An Analogy on Expectations ... 49
   Moment of Truth ... 50
   A Trauma – Informed Approach ... 51

Chapter 5 — Stealing Away 15 Minutes ... 55
   Moment of Truth ... 58

Chapter 6 — Connecting to Your Child's Heart	67
Moment of Truth 75	
Chapter 7 — Growing Resilient Hearts	77
Moment of Truth..81	
Chapter 8 — Mastering Meltdown Moments	83
Moment of Truth..92	
Chapter 9 — The Journey to Mended Hearts	93
Stepping Outside the Book 96	
Letter from the Author	99

Introduction

Thank you for being here, prioritizing yourself and your family, and being open to trying something different. Despite my gratitude for your presence, you need to know that I wrote this book for myself. This is the book that I needed on so many occasions. My bookshelves are lined with parenting books, child development books, trauma resources, and more. In moments when I needed the most support, skimming through multiple books was time-consuming. Let's be honest: who has time to read seventeen different books on parenting?

If you are anything like I was, you are here because you are tired! You have received advice, suggestions, and recommendations from everyone you know. Community leaders and pastors offer advice on old fashioned, "what worked for me" ways for reducing defiance. Your parents and other elders in the family have great suggestions on what helped another family member when they were "that age." And of course, professionals like teachers and mental health counselors, have offered many recommendations for behavior modification and structure. And yet you are still here, there is still something missing, and *I am glad this book found you!*

All of that great advice and insight seems like it worked wonders for others and really turned their lives around, but it does not feel applicable to your situation or your child. You see there is something special and unique about you and your child's relationship that people tend to overlook. The obstacles in your relationship with them are different than other parent-child relationships. Many people fail to grasp that, despite the love, attention, and stability you've provided, there's still the elephant in the room — the awareness that you may not be their first parent or birth parent.

Being a foster and/or adoptive parent comes with an implicit disadvantage — the inability to establish a secure attachment from the womb. The parent-child relationship is often overlooked as something that must be cultivated and created. Foster and adoptive parents often meet your child when they have already been wounded and traumatized in many ways. The most crucial takeaway from this book is the significance of nurturing and intentionally growing your relationship with your child. Dedicate time to getting to know your child — their likes, dislikes, dreams, and fears — throughout all stages of their lives. Should you decide to put this book down now and never read another page, remember to develop the relationship.

My impact is to empower foster and adoptive parents to navigate meltdown moments by addressing

trauma and behavior science, allowing them to have a better relationship and rediscover the joy of parenting.

Dealing with a child showing defiant behavior can make it a challenge to be around them, for yourself and others, due to the ongoing battle of behaviors. The purpose of this book is to empower you, as it has me, to be able to have a good relationship with your child, even with defiant behaviors; even with a trauma history, even if not biologically yours. If you are being honest with others and yourself, parenting a child is tough and exhausting work. Parenting a child with defiant behavior makes the job feel 10x harder. Maybe you have been on the brink of giving up; feeling like it would be easier to just "let someone else raise them," "find a placement until they outgrow this phase," or "just let the world teach them." I want to offer encouragement that all the tough times have led you here, in this moment, with me – on a journey to transform behaviors.

INTRODUCTION

This book isn't about right or wrong, good or bad, perfect or imperfect parenting. **This book is designed to be a conversation from one parent to another on parenting challenges through defiant behaviors with some encouraging words.** My journey may be a little different because I work as a licensed professional counselor who is a trauma and child's behavior expert. But I am also a parent who is learning along the way.

My aim for this book is to offer education, insights, and perspective on parenting that provide support, encouragement, and opportunities of self-growth. I want you to journey with me, parent-to-parent, as you explore the complex behaviors in children, unique issues facing foster and adoptive families, and the role trauma plays in defiance. I will also offer insights and strategies to help establish better relationships within families. To increase the impact, there will be opportunities for self-reflection, personal discovery, and growth during this journey. The opportunity is yours and this work is very personal but necessary.

Allow me to introduce you to four important aspects of the book:

Cassie and Isabelle take center stage in this book. I have woven their journey from the foster care system to adoption throughout. Their story is the shared experience of so many children and families.

The **Moment of Truth** will appear in various sections of this book. Serving as a time for self-discovery, my aim is for you to step away from the book, get your pencil and paper or your digital notepad and answer the questions honestly and self-reflectively. These reflections will guide how you understand the information, interpret it, and apply it to your everyday parenting journey.

Stepping Outside the Book encompasses the practical and interactive elements of this book. Inspired by the concept of stepping outside the box, these activities are experiential and put into action what we've discussed. Set aside time to actively engage in the activities described in the "Consider This" section. Some of these activities may require creative materials like markers, colored pencils, crayons, and paper; so be prepared to explore your creativity.

Self-Paced Companion Guide invites you to continue your exploration and growth thorough additional insights, activities, and reflections. They are designed to accompany you as you apply the concepts from this book in your daily life. Accessing this guide is simple and comes at no extra cost with your purchase of this book. It's my way of extending my support beyond these pages.

> Register for the Self-Paced Companion Guide at www.meganmhamm.com/the-heart-of-the-matter

Meet Cassie and Isabelle

Cassie, an excited, insightful, and highly motivated foster mother, has just met another piece of her heart. Despite being absolute strangers, a common occurrence in the foster care system, Isabelle instantly became a part of Cassie's family. Cassie dug into stories and child protective reports about Isabelle's trauma history and her disruptive home placements. Determined to make this placement work, Cassie vowed not to be abusive, providing stability and offering all the love a child could ask for, want, or need. And so, the journey begins.

Chapter 1

The Heart of Meltdown Moments

> *"In the middle of difficulty, there lies opportunity"*
> — Albert Einstein

Let's dive into defining and understanding defiant behaviors. This is not meant to label your child or their experiences but to ensure you're on the same page about the behaviors I'm discussing. For definition purposes, defiant behaviors are categorized as disruptive, lack of self-control, and/or behavior issues.

Defiant behavior shows up as:

- The child who fails or refuses to follow directions,
- The child who argues with other children and adults,
- The child who purposely annoys others,
- The child who "can dish it out but can't take it",
- The child who gets angry easily,
- The child who blames everybody else for their mistakes or behaviors.

Defiant behavior can lead to problems in children such as:

- not getting along with other children or making friends,
- not doing well with working on a team,
- having trouble getting along with family members,
- isolating the parent from other adult support,
- displaying disruptive behaviors at school.

Three factors impact the development of defiant behaviors:

Developmental – The defiant behaviors begin in early childhood during the toddler years. They have difficulty solving problems due to their emotional attachment to another person.

Environmental – Defiant behaviors are a product of the living environment and family life and are typically learned behavior.

Medical – Defiant behaviors can develop as a response to childhood physical illness and disease.

When understanding defiant behaviors, there are more layers to the onion of complexity with adopted and foster children. The behavior may be perceived as disrespectful, disobedient, or rebellious. It is important to understand at this point these behaviors can stem from underlying issues of trauma, negative interactions with others, and/or lack of stability in the foster care system. The defiant behaviors can also serve the purpose of safety, security, and survival for children whose lives have been impacted by trauma.

Children who have been through the foster care system, even if adopted, have had traumatic experiences that have changed how they regulate their emotions. These meltdown moments can reflect a lack of connection to positive relationships - which leads to struggles with trusting others, feeling safe in relationships, and managing their moods. The foster care system can be an indirect source of unstable living conditions such as moving through multiple foster care placements which compounds the traumatic experience.

The goal of this chapter is not to make excuses for defiant behavior but to understand it differently. It is the goal to identify that life's experiences such as trauma, issues with attachment, and multiple foster placements may increase defiant behaviors.

These defiant behaviors may be complex and can be symptoms of underlying issues. You can change and challenge your current approach by understanding how trauma can be the root cause and the behaviors are a response to their past situations.

After this chapter, the behaviors will not be referred to as defiance, oppositional, or disrespectful — but you're shifting your perspective and recognizing them as "meltdown moments." I am specific and intentional in saying moments because I want you to understand that although it may not feel like it, the behaviors last for moments at a time. Doesn't *moment* feel like something that won't last long, will be over soon, or something you can become a master of? If you agree, then so do I.

You heard this throughout the entire foster and adoption process. You were prepared for through your completion of numerous hours of foster parent training to help you understand the potential for defiant behaviors and your role in supporting this child. You were also advised to integrate this child into your home and "treat them like they were yours."

> Visit www.meganmhamm.com/the-heart-of-the-matter to learn more about the language shift from defiance to meltdown moments.

Moment of Truth

Remember to step away from the book, get your pencil and paper or your digital notepad and answer the questions honestly and with the purpose of self-discovery.

- What does it truly mean to "treat them like they were yours?
- Have you ever had any parent training/class? What did you learn that was helpful? What did you wish you had learned?
- What has your experience been with defiant behaviors as a parent (birth, foster, and/or adoptive)?
- Is defiant and disrespectful behavior different for foster and adoptive children compared to children of birth?
- How do you manage the behaviors of children in the home with different upbringings?

Chapter 2

The Brain and Heart Connection

"The heart knows what the mind can't explain"
—Author Unknown

It is a 'no-brainer' that many foster and adoptive children have experienced trauma. I want to challenge our current ideals of who is identified as an adopted or foster child. For this book, I will refer to adopted or foster child as any child who is not being raised in the home by at least one primary birth parent. This definition includes familial placements (such as sister, cousin, uncle, or aunt) and grandparents raising grandchildren.

Trauma can look like everything and nothing all at once. This means trauma can impact an individual in various ways that may mimic other medical and mental health diagnoses. It also means it can feel like nothing because it is so subjective that it may not look like anything you have seen before.

Examples of trauma that I have heard over the years:

- physical and sexual abuse,
- neglect,
- not having relationships with parents/feeling ignored,
- being in the foster care system,
- living in a household with an adult with mental health issues,
- substance use within the household,
- experiencing a significant loss,
- lack of safety in the community,

- trauma associated with race, age, and gender,
- being ignored or the black sheep of the family.

Many adopted or foster children may have experienced several traumas from this list, and this can continue over the next several pages, highlighting the subjective nature of trauma and traumatic experiences.

When assessing for trauma, my rule of thumb is not to assume or expect a certain symptom, behavior, response, or outcome. I allow parents to tell me what they are currently or have experienced, and I honor those experiences.

> Isabelle's traumatic experiences were something Cassie had no personal experience with; Isabelle had already endured four known traumas that led to her placement in foster care, not to mention the chronic trauma of being a child in foster care. Isabelle was 2 years old when placed in foster care. For the 29 months she was in custody, she was still expected to meet developmental, social-emotional, and academic milestones on the same level as her peers. She was expected to adjust to the environments, go to school, and "act right." This was difficult for Isabelle and her responses to her instability, safety, and trauma were –

disruptive and defiant. She was defiant in preschool, she was defiant in the foster home, she was defiant at community events. The solution to her defiance – placement disruption is to find a "more suitable home" or "a therapeutic home." The ongoing defiant behaviors caused numerous placement disruptions, being removed from familial caregivers and support, and forced to establish rapport and relationship with over eight case managers. By the time she met Cassie, the only consistency in her last 29 months was her judge, whom she had only met 1 time. In all honesty, Isabelle was tired. She had tried her best to make sense of her world and most times when she struggled, she was removed, to start over again. The moves became farther and farther from her family of origin. It was on a rainy Wednesday evening when Isabelle met Cassie. Although she could not form the words, she understood what meeting someone new meant and yet again, she was forced to figure it out.

As a parent, especially a foster or adoptive parent, understanding brain and childhood development is the entrance to a secret world. In this world, each emotion and behavior seem to make sense. **Every behavior is a language in itself.** If I had to rank it over the last 16 years in service, the #1 question asked by parents is,

"Is this normal?" "Is this something they will grow out of with age? Or maturity?"

Have you ever watched a movie or read a book, and the character was a child impacted by trauma? If you have, and if the script or book was well written – you were able to experience the trauma with them, how they navigated their internal struggles, as well as how the trauma showed in their behaviors. You could understand it better because you were aware of the internal aspects. How many of the children you know who can express their internal parts? If it's anything like my experiences, the answer to why is usually a shoulder shrug, an unconvincing - 'I don't know,' or no response at all. Their internal struggles are mostly hidden from them, as well as us. These internal struggles, hidden triggers, and unseen battles become all too real for foster and adoptive children.

Let's start by saying I am not a neuroscientist, brain expert, or anything else you feel may qualify me to impart knowledge on how the brain works. But I am a person who has dug deep to figure out the missing piece is brain science. **Understanding the brain is key to unlocking behavior.** I proudly tell anyone who would listen that I am 'in recovery from behavior modification.' It was my thing, something I excelled at; I studied it and became the best behavior modifier that I knew. It was my life's work (not really) until I discovered that it was just band-aiding the issue and hoping the band-aid would stay long enough for the child to grow out of it. So, in my personal quest to find something that would last longer, I discovered the neurobiology of behavior. That's a fancy way to say understanding how behavior works by understanding the brain.

The brain is the central organ that shapes your experiences of the world. Every action, emotion, and response have to go through the brain. Understanding the brain's basic functions helps you to recognize why your child has certain behaviors, especially if your child has been affected by traumatic experiences. It is widely researched that trauma impacts the brain's development and keeps it from fully developing in different areas. The areas that are not fully developed impact the parts of the brain that may cause learning disabilities and increased behaviors.

> Learn more about trauma's impact on the brain at www.meganmhamm.com/the-heart-of-the-matter.

Trauma and the Catch-All Closet

I can remember growing up, there was a catch-all or storage closet in our living room. This was the closet or space in the house where random things were stored that didn't have a designated space. I can remember that everything ended up in the living room closet —from out-of-season sports equipment to Christmas trees and ornaments, to one-time-use sleeping bags. As a child, I hated searching for something in the closet or being responsible for putting something in the closet. As soon as I opened the door, most — if not all — of the contents would fall at my feet; then it became a headache to get it back in, so I just stuffed it in, shut the door fast, and hoped I wouldn't be the next person to have to open the door again.

Think of the brain as the catch-all closet where each traumatic experience is stored. In the trauma-impacted brain, memories and content are just thrown into the closet — unorganized, with no specific place to be kept, forced to fit into whatever open space or crevice was available. When something happens, i.e. being redirected, meeting a new person, having a meltdown moment, it is like someone opening the closet door and everything falls onto the floor. In this child, you see the mess on the floor (meltdown moments) but you don't realize there is a door, let alone an closet of stuff.

The child's trauma connects the brain to their behavior. A child's behavior is a language – it speaks to their brain's function and how they make sense of the world. As a society, it's important to move away from the thought process that children "want" or "choose" or "manipulate" with meltdown moments.

> *"The parenting role is not to change the child's behaviors – your role is to recognize and manage trauma responses so that you can change how you respond and support your child."*

Imagine the traumas in the catch-all closet can't be thrown away. Your response to your child can help to organize the closet so that it won't all fall out on the floor whenever the door is open.

Cassie and Isabelle dived right into the deep end of trauma-responsive behaviors. There was no warning, a honeymoon phase, or a time to "get to know each other." From the first night in the home, Isabelle struggled with emotional regulation. She cried and screamed for three hours when Cassie asked her to take a bath. She simply refused to get in the tub. Cassie thought it was best to allow her to go to her room and get some sleep. Sleep is always a good solution, Cassie thought. Isabelle woke up during the night crying and screaming. She refused to be comforted (hugged), she refused for Cassie to enter the room, and she cried even louder when Cassie walked out of the room. Nothing was off limits for Isabelle. Anything in her room that was not too heavy to lift was thrown about the room. Cassie was trying to be empathetic, understanding, and trauma-informed, but it just felt like too much. Well, maybe she'll come around after a few days of feeling stable, loving Isabelle, and showing connection and compassion. As Isabelle and Cassie finally went to bed exhausted, Cassie knew tomorrow would be better.

Cassie and Isabelle still attempt to navigate these outbursts three weeks later with patience and prayer. At this point, Cassie has some understanding of child development and the developing brain. It was not extensive, and she could not talk about it for 10 minutes, but she could get through a conversation. It was hard for her to breathe and consider Isabelle's brain development because she was putting out daily fires of outbursts. Cassie was up one night, googling, researching, and trying to figure out what to do, when she came across a poster about the brain science of behaviors. Cassie made the page her favorite, closed the computer, and slept. She was exhausted - she would figure out what that meant for Isabelle – but that had to wait until tomorrow.

Moment of Truth

Remember to step away from the book, get your pencil and paper or your digital notepad and answer the questions honestly and with the purpose of self-discovery.

- How would you have responded to Isabelle's first night?

- Would you have contacted her case worker about her placement after the first night?

- Do you think her behaviors were intentional or a trauma response? Why or why not?

- What do you think Isabelle's behaviors were communicating?

- How did you think Cassie did? Is there anything she could have done differently?

Parenting R + R

Parenting R + R is the concept that parenting includes having a relationship with self + a relationship with the child. If either of these components of the parent-child relationship are missing or struggling, then there is very little R + R and the parenting journey can become difficult. In this book, I focus on the relationship with self as the first part of the parenting journey in Chapters 3, 4, and 5. The relationship with your child is as equally important and further explored in Chapters 6, 7, and 8.

Relationship with Self

The relationship with self is the part of the parenting journey where you learn about yourself. In this stage of self-discovery there are elements of self-reflection to guide you through your own personal journey of parenthood. The parent-child relationship has two components – the parent and the child. I believe that the parent component is your relationship with self and debatably, the most important part of it. During this discovery stage, you will focus on your parenting journey, expectations as a parent, and self-care. **Every parent must discover self before they can create, maintain, or transform a relationship with their child.**

Relationship with Child

Relationship with a child is the next component of the parent-child relationship. Too often, you have focused your relationship with your child based on being able to provide for them – a stable home, food, love, and structure. I believe all of these are very important, but I also feel there is something special and unique about the relationship. It is the art of getting to know your child - their likes and dislikes, how you can have fun together, and what is important to them. During this portion of the book, you will focus on building a relationship with your children, managing the meltdown moments, and ways to help them be resilient. **Connection is the foundation of healing.**

Cassie is a very motivated foster parent. She was raised in a loving home with both parents and siblings. She has always been a caretaker, babysitting at the early age of 13. She was always seen as responsible, and family members trusted her with her younger cousins. Cassie had always dreamed of being a mother, raising a family, and doing all the things that "fun moms" did. She envisioned being active in PTA, baking cookies, snuggling for movie nights, and eating popcorn. Cassie would dream of mommy dates, dance parties, and dressing up for character days at school. When she met her husband, she felt like becoming a mother was the natural path. Cassie and her husband struggled with fertility issues, which became a stressor for Cassie. It was the first thing she had failed at in life that she couldn't just try to be better at doing. Fostering and adopting had always been something she was aware of and had dreamed about – she didn't know it would be her only path to motherhood. After spending years praying with her husband to foster, Cassie and her spouse intentionally began their journey to parenthood, planning and preparing for what they believed would be an awesome experience.

Chapter 3

The Heart of Parenting

"Strive to become the parent you want your children to remember for a lifetime"
— Author Unknown

Let's explore the journey into parenthood. While there are various paths to becoming a parent, your love and care for your child unite you more than your differences. **Parenting is an uncharted journey with abundant rewards.** This is the opportunity to fully explore your parenting journey. Trauma-informed does not mean that you are blaming the child's behavior on trauma and doing nothing about it; it means you understand that trauma impacts their behaviors, and your responses must be different. By prioritizing an understanding, you can adopt a different approach to the meltdown moments.

Nurturing a child who has faced trauma alters your perspective on parenting. To be honest, dealing with continuous meltdown moments, lack of accountability, and argumentative behavior can make the joy of parenting disappear. Parenting can feel like the most daunting job you have ever had with the least rewards. Your child doesn't always know or understand the sacrifices made as parents only for them to sometimes make you feel like you are not doing it well. Recall the discussion about the catch-all closet; your role is to organize the chaos, minimizing the chances of everything collapsing at once and being there as a support for your child when it does.

When you are parenting a child with meltdowns that can show up anywhere - at home, school, grocery store, or church - you get tired of dealing with it. You love your child, but sometimes you don't like to be around them, and you start to feel more and more comfortable with them just being in another room. The child being in another room becomes easy, but it does not fulfill the vision you had of parenting and parenthood. It does not reflect baking cookies, laughing together, and watching movies with popcorn. If you, as a parent, have ever contemplated giving up due to overwhelming behaviors, here's a tip— let your heart guide you in building a stronger relationship with your child. If your heart leads, it will be easier to see the behaviors decrease. **I want you to return to having a better relationship with your child and rediscover the joy of parenting.**

Currently, it might seem like the ups are few or they rarely happen. I am here to reassure you that more ups are possible. Honesty and clarity about your parenthood journey will help you discover and be more intentional in how you choose to be a parent. The fact that you are this far in the book and still interested in learning more says a lot about the type of parent you want to be and your willingness to learn and try something different.

Moment of Truth

Remember to step away from the book, get your pencil and paper or your digital notepad and answer the questions honestly and with the purpose of self-discovery.

- How did you navigate the tough times in your parenting journey? Celebrate your victories?

- What has been your motivation for having children? Fostering children? Adopting children? Or being a parent?

- Did you ever dream about what type of parent you wanted to be?

- How has dealing with your child's meltdown moments changed your parenting vision?

- What can you do to be a better parent than you were yesterday?

Stepping Outside the Book

The following activities are crafted to assist you in honing your goals and gaining clarity on your journey into parenthood – envisioning the parent you aspire to be and the parent you aim to become.

> Access the toolkit for
> Chapter 3's Stepping Outside the Book at
> www.meganmhamm.com/the-heart-of-the-matter

1. **Create a parenting vision statement**: Define your current vision of the parent you aspire to be. How has this vision evolved since you first became a parent?

2. **Parent your inner child**: Reflect on whether you are the parent you wished for at your child's age? Identify both the similarities and differences. Recall a recent behavioral scenario of your child – envision

yourself in their situation and describe how you, as the parent, would have responded. How did it feel to parent yourself? What did you know about yourself and the internal dialogue that would change how you responded as a parent?

3. **Future child**: Write a letter to your child in the future, 5-10-15 years from now. Congratulate them on the aspirations of where you think they are, the type of life they are living, and the goals they have set and reached for themselves. Reflect on a most trying time during your parenting journey with them, offer insight into your rationale and thinking for how you responded, explain your internal struggles with being their parent, and tell them how you overcame them.

Chapter 4

Healing the Heart from Expectation

"Expectation is the root of all heartache"
— *William Shakespeare*

You have set expectations for yourself, others, and the world. You anticipate that certain things will unfold just as you envision or believe they should. In the preceding chapter, your focus was on self-discovery and exploring your desired parental identity. In this chapter, you delve into setting realistic expectations for your child, embracing their imperfections, and introducing the concept of trauma-informed parenting.

Parenting, especially for foster and adoptive parents, blurs the line between your aspirations and reality. You navigate the delicate balance of appreciating your child's imperfection and having expectations of how you want them to behave. Your vision of parent and/or parenthood is often the opposite of the chaotic realities, which are the trauma responses of your child's behaviors.

> Cassie and her spouse are "all in" with their parenting role. Isabelle is adjusting to being in the home setting and really dealing with some major meltdown moments. Both parents understand how trauma plays a role in how she sees the world and responds but they also thought that they can love and support the trauma out of her. Being honest with themselves, they wonder, the longer she is in the home and the more she sees their care and love, shouldn't the behaviors stop? By the six-month mark, she should have been in the house long enough to recognize their love and let her behaviors reflect that. Cassie grappled with the expectations Isabelle would behave better simply because she was loved. After

six months in the home, Isabelle's foster parents, like many parents, were expecting peaceful mornings, family dinners filled with laughter and stories of the day, and a child who responded knowing they were understood and loved. The reality of foster parenting was rushed mornings that were complete with meltdowns and school tardies, family dinners that were non-existent due to time outs and early bedtimes, and unexpected emotional outbursts that remain unexplained.

I can imagine that you have had a similar experience among parents who are navigating the double-edged sword that is their aspirations and their realities of behavior. Give yourself grace, you are learning. **Every challenging moment with your child hides an opportunity to grow closer, to understand deeper. Embrace these moments, for they become the foundation of your parenting journey.**

As a parent, you probably hold a vision of perfection (or something really close to it) at the heart of your parenting, a dream of raising your child without fault or failure. You know in your mind and soul that perfection is an illusion. There is a fear that your imperfection as a parent, your "just not good enough," your "I tried my best" will not be enough to raise a healthy, whole, and productive child. The perfect parent does not exist. The parent *who is trying their best* exists. The parent *who is striving to be better today than yesterday* exists. The parent *who is choosing to read this book to learn something different* exists. As a parent, you are learning and growing every day – as your child is also evolving into a different person. Parenting a six-year-old differs from parenting a sixteen-year-old, despite the ten years of experience in between.

On this parenting journey, I want you to be able to acknowledge and accept imperfections. This doesn't mean lowering your standards of behavior or giving up on the dreams you have for your child. Instead, it involves recognizing that parenting is an unpredictable journey that is as much about learning and growing as it is about teaching and guiding.

Trauma-informed parenting is the idea that as a parent, there are times where you will take into account your child's trauma history into your parenting techniques and responses. Foster and adoptive children who have experienced trauma often show meltdown moments that are misunderstood or challenging. As a parent, you must be able to separate yourself from your child's behavior. These behaviors are not reflections of parental failure but are signals of the deep emotional and psychological impact of their past experiences. **Committing to your heart, not just words in your head, empathy and understanding are needed in accepting imperfections in your child.** I often remind countless parents that your child is constantly learning – they are trying to figure out how to navigate life and make sense of their world. During this time, they won't be perfect and will make many mistakes. Your role is to support and guide them in learning from those mistakes.

Balanced expectations form the foundation for accepting imperfections in your child. The expectations allow you, as a parent, to set realistic goals for yourself and your child. Progress for behaviors, especially in the context of trauma, is a gradual process. **This balance is not about diminishing hope or aspiration; it's about meeting them where they are and being able to stay with them as long as they need you.** It's about understanding that each day may not bring monumental changes, but small steps towards healing and growth.

> Visit www.meganmhamm.com/the-heart-of-the-matter to explore more on parenting expectations.

An Analogy on Expectations

As a human, you most likely have an expectation for everything that is done in your life. You expect people to act a certain way and you expect outcomes. These expectations guide your decisions and lead you to anticipate what will happen. You must make your expectations realistic based on evidence and not always based on aspirations. **Unrealistic expectations are like standing under an apple tree, waiting for an orange to fall.** Persisting in expecting the orange will only result in ongoing disappointment. If you accept the sweetness of the apple, you will have a better experience.

The parenting journey of a foster and adoptive parent is about embracing the unpredictable, telling the difference between aspirational and realistic expectations and ultimately finding peace in the beautiful chaos of parenting. You need to be able to manage expectations and transform them into a source of strength and resilience.

Moment of Truth

Remember to step away from the book, get your pencil and paper or your digital notepad and answer the questions honestly and with the purpose of self-discovery.

- What are your expectations for your child? Are they realistic or aspirational? And what lead you to answer either way?
- What do you expect from your children's home, school, and community behaviors?
- The behaviors that you expect in your children, would you be able to meet those expectations as a child? How was it for you? What helped you to meet or not meet the expectations?

Is there a difference between your ideal parenting scenario and your daily experience as a parent? What parts align, and which ones do not?

A Trauma – Informed Approach

Trauma-informed parenting has three main components—understanding, empathy, and adaptability. A myth about trauma-informed parenting is that it gives an excuse for the meltdown moments of your child. It is less about excuse-giving and more about recognizing the deep-seated impact of past traumas on your child's behavior and responding with sensitivity and care. This approach challenges some traditional parenting techniques and how you were parented. It moves towards intentional ways of responding to meltdown moments of your child that acknowledge the unique needs of your child's trauma.

Traditional parenting methods may often leave you feeling overwhelmed by your child's emotional outbursts and meltdown moments. Many foster and adoptive parents face similar situations marked by confusion, frustration, and, sometimes, a sense of helplessness. Trauma-informed parenting principles will help you see your child's behavior in a new light. As a parent, you learn that their actions are not simply acts of defiance or emotional instability but how their trauma shows up in their world. These behaviors are often survival strategies that your child has developed to cope with their traumatic experiences. This understanding is a turning point for transforming your parenting approach. Recognizing this, you can approach your child's behaviors with empathy rather than frustration.

Trauma-informed approach helps you to create a safe and stable environment for your child. The primary function of a foster and adoptive parent is to provide a safe and stable environment. You provide a space where your child can feel secure, valued, and understood. You create consistent routines, clear communication, and set boundaries with kindness and respect. This is the environment where your child can begin to heal from their past traumas and develop healthier ways of expressing their emotions and needs. Remember, being a trauma-informed parent is not about perfection but about progress.

    Cassie felt like she had tried every parenting– gentle, peaceful, playful, positive, shame-proof, Christian, strict, and easy-going. However, she felt like nothing was changing in Isabelle's behavior; she actually felt like the behavior had worsened. The outbursts were happening just as often at home and sometimes lasted longer. Finding consequences and sticking to the discipline she agreed on with her husband had become harder. At this point, they were trying to get the tantrums to stop. Isabelle resorted to destroying her toys and room, tearing up clothes, and punching holes in the wall whenever she was told no or wanted to get her way. Cassie and her husband were at the end of their road. They understood the role that trauma played in the behaviors and worked hard to understand it. Still, it did not make it any easier to deal with the behaviors. Cassie and her husband were worn out – always on edge, agitated, and short with each other. It was hard to get childcare because no one else would handle her. At this point in the journey, four long months have passed with no breaks. Adjusting from no children in the home to constant outbursts was beginning to take a toll on them individually and their marriage.

The challenge for you is, "How to remain consistent, clear, safe, and stable when the chaos of the meltdown moments is constant, unpredictable, and overwhelming?"

Chapter 5

Stealing Away 15 Minutes

"Caring for myself is not self-indulgence, it is self-preservation"

— Audre Lorde

Parenting children with meltdown moments, particularly in foster and adoptive situations, can be both rewarding and challenging, requiring significant emotional, physical, and mental energy. Recognizing the critical role of self-care for both the parent and the parenting relationship is essential. **Self-care is the concept of caring for self.** Self-care is about intentionally taking care of self—engaging in practices about self in order.

Parenting with the complexities of trauma can be emotionally taxing, and without proper care, parents can experience burnout. Parental burnout is a feeling of being overwhelmed, stressed out, and exhausted. Burnout can be physical, mental, and/or emotional exhaustion. What does it look like to confide in someone that you have parenting fatigue? How do you share with someone that you are exhausted as a parent? Would you admit to someone that being a parent is emotionally draining? Most of you will answer NO. You may not even share these things with a therapist or other support. You try to keep it all together and pretend you are doing fine and enjoying being a parent. It is important to recognize when you are experiencing burnout as a parent.

Consider the some of the following burnout symptoms:

- Not wanting to be bothered by your child or anyone else,
- Always irritated and yelling,
- Feeling stressed and overwhelmed,
- Constant complaints of headaches and other aches and pains,
- Feelings of resentment, shame, or guilt about how you parent.

Moment of Truth

Remember to step away from the book, get your pencil and paper or your digital notepad and answer the questions honestly and with the purpose of self-discovery.

- Within the last 2 weeks, have you felt any of the symptoms from the burnout list?
- Are there any symptoms you would add to the list?
- Did you recognize the symptoms as burnout?
- What does self-care mean to you? What does your current self-care routine consist of?

Acknowledging burnout is self-awareness that is crucial for recognizing the need for self-care. Self-care involves granting yourself permission to be self-aware. The more you allow yourself permission to engage in self-care.

Three tools to improve your self-awareness and prevent burnout:

Celebrate your progress: The progress can be small tasks such as going to the gym, asking for support for your child, or buying take-out without guilt.

Set boundaries for self and others: Setting boundaries is another important concept in self-care awareness. Sometimes you just need to be able and willing to say no.

Accept your current situation: As a parent, dealing with your child's meltdown behaviors, it is important to accept where you are in your life and on your parenting journey. Acceptance is not about giving an excuse but more importantly, understanding where you are and what you may need on your parenting journey.

There are several myths about self-care that probably keep you from making it a priority in your parenting journey. You have gotten messages from society that once you become a parent, your child becomes your life's priority. Your child does become your responsibility; although, their wants, needs, and desires should not become more important than yours. You often prioritize others and allocate to yourself only what is "leftover." I am here to tell you that this approach contradicts what is needed for you to be the best version of yourself as a parent. Parenting can mean giving so much of yourself to your child and family, leaving very little for you. It is also said that self-care is an act of selfishness, there is not enough time for it, and it is a luxury. I am challenging that thought process and want to tell you the truth about self-care. The truth is self-care is not selfish. It should be prioritized, and is necessary as an individual, especially as a parent. Self-care allows you as a parent to recharge and approach your parenting responsibilities with renewed energy and patience. In talking to many parents, the biggest difficulty in self-care is having enough time. To better care for your child, you must first take care of self – that is self-care.

Three steps to be intentional about self-care:

Step 1: **Prioritize self-care** – I can only imagine the care and consideration you take with your work schedule, child's appointments, and the requests of everyone around you. Suppose you have a scheduled day off to take your child to an appointment. Would someone else be able to add another task simultaneously? Probably not, since you have prioritized the time and understand it's importance. Prioritizing self-care means putting the same level of importance on your self-care activities that you would place on an appointment for your child.

Step 2: **Schedule the time** – Be intentional with scheduling the time on your schedule. Identify the best times for you with minimal distractions. It may sound good to say that I will get up at 5 am to meditate and have "me time," but the way my life is set up, I don't know what 5 am looks like. As a busy parent, my optimal time is during the day between work and my children's activities or in the evening after the children's bedtime. Does that sound familiar? Find the time that is the best for you and your schedule. I don't want you to set yourself up for failure by scheduling something you won't be able to commit the time on your schedule.

Step 3: **Stealing away 15 minutes** – Stealing away 15 minutes means dedicating 15 minutes daily to do something for yourself. This activity, experience, and /or hobby should bring joy and relaxation. It can last more than 15 minutes but 15 minutes is the minimum. You say all the time that 15 minutes is not enough but think about how a quick 15 minute nap transformed your life when your child was an infant or 15 minutes of peace and quiet when your toddler learned how to play by themselves. I want you to think about what are some ways that you can incorporate 15-minute self-care increments into your daily schedule. These 15 minutes of self-care will be simple, quick, and impactful.

> Visit www.meganmhamm.com/the-heart-of-the-matter to download 15 Quick Self-Care Practices for Busy Parents

Cassie has found herself in a never-ending cycle of caring for others – at home, at work, and in the community. Her days are filled with meetings, parent-teacher conferences, and the emotional labor of supporting children who have faced more in their few years than many do in a lifetime. This has become the backdrop to Cassie's life. Her own needs – a quiet cup of coffee, time to read (or listen to) a book, or even a moment of solitude – become distant memories. It felt like it was easier for her husband to get time alone because some of the everyday tasks he had to do were not designed for a little girl – going to the gym, the barber shop, or hanging with the fellas. It seems like his routine activities are taking longer and longer. Cassie decided she needed to take her self-care into her own hands. She enrolled Isabelle in an after-school program, giving Cassie 30 minutes after work before she had to pick her up. She and her husband decided to take Isabelle on daughter dates once per week. When it was Cassie's turn, she and Isabelle would leave the house and do something fun for about 2 hours – to give her husband some solitude at home. And he would do the same for her. They ensured the activities were enjoyable for Isabelle to minimize the chances of an outburst. The park near their home and ice cream became something everyone looked forward to each week. They were sure to make sure it had nothing to do with behavior but just a time to build attachment and relationship with each other. Cassie woke up 30 minutes earlier than Isabelle every morning and could once again savor a cup of coffee in her cozy robe and warm socks. After the last sip, she would smile, take a deep breath, and prepare her mind for the day.

Chapter 6

Connecting to Your Child's Heart

"The most important things in life are the connections you make with others"
— Tom Ford

Every person has an innate need for connection and belonging. The desire to feel valued, needed and loved is profound. It's important to recognize that these feelings are not solely shaped by your words but by the actions and experiences you share with others. As Maya Angelou eloquently said, "I've learned that people will forget what you said, people will forget what you did, but people will never forget how you made them feel." Foster and adopted children grapple with overwhelming and sometimes bewildering emotions related to connection and belonging. Forming bonds and trusting others can be challenging for them, considering past experiences that taught them connection leads to hurt and disappointment.

>Cassie is discovering that her most potent tool for Isabelle is her presence. Every night, Cassie follows a routine of tucking Isabelle into bed. Isabelle's responses vary – sometimes triggering another meltdown and sometimes seeking connection. Undeterred by the meltdowns, Cassie decides to remain consistent in her actions. On a specific night, following a meltdown about bath time, Cassie discovers Isabelle in her closet, softly whimpering. Cassie, facing blank mind and lacking words, chooses not to be frustrated. Instead, she sits in the closet with Isabelle, offering a presence of calm, connection, and understanding. Isabelle rests her head on Cassie's shoulder, crying for about 30 minutes. With no words or glances exchanged, Isabelle eventually rises, gives Cassie a hug and kiss, and softly utters, "I love you, Mama." Cassie replies, "I love you too," they both head

to bed. Cassie recognizes that her seemingly inactive response was the most appropriate action.

One challenging aspect is working on building (or rebuilding) a relationship with someone when it's filled with meltdown moments, conflict, and stress. This is when forgiveness becomes crucial, and the focus should shift towards building, re-building, and re-re-building the relationship. The power dynamic inherent in the parent-child relationship makes it harder for you, as a parent, to recognize the significance of building that connection. Truly understanding your child, engaging in enjoyable experiences, and finding joy in being their parent and relishing in their presence as an individual are essential. A common misconception is that, as a parent, you must enforce strict boundaries and structure with your child experiencing meltdown moments. Some believe being too nice or lenient will lead to your child not taking you seriously or manipulating you. This is unequivocally NOT TRUE.

You can have a relationship that is both fun, loving and structured with your child. It's crucial to realize that every shared moment is a step towards healing and growth.

I want to focus on three intentional ways to build (or rebuild) the relationship with your child: making meaningful memories, open communication, and unconditional acceptance.

Making Meaningful Memories: Building bonds through shared experiences is key to connecting with a child, especially one with a history of trauma. Recall your childhood, and you likely remember a memorable moment with your family, whether planned (like a family vacation) or spontaneous (like a funny dinner incident). In these simple yet profound moments, barriers of distrust and trauma dissolve, paving the way for memories that can weather any storm. It's crucial to intentionally select activities to do together, resonating with you and your child. It can involve trying something new. These memories may include taking a sewing class, swinging at the park, or dedicating a day to painting and crafts. Each activity should be an adventure, not focusing on life's obligations but on having fun and making memories. Allowing your child to choose some activities provides them a sense of control and partnership, fostering an understanding that their interests, joys, and presence matter. Scheduling these meaningful memories should be consistent and distraction-free, ensuring undivided attention. The time together becomes a safe space where everyone can let their guard down and they can simply be in a child's place. Regularity is more than a routine; it's a reassurance – a constant in a life that might have been filled with uncertainties. Meaningful memories serve as a bridge to your child's heart, establishing the foundation for a deep and trusted connection that supports healing and growth.

> Access the download on being intentional with meaningful memories at www.meganmhamm.com/the-heart-of-the-matter.

Open Communication: You've all heard about open communication, know its importance, and understand how it makes you feel. However, defining it can be elusive, often easier to describe what it is not that what it is. Open communication isn't your child telling you anything at any time; yet, in a way, it is. Communication takes center stage when building a trusting relationship with an adopted or foster child. In all honesty, communication is crucial in all your relationships. It's more than just words; it's about creating an environment where your child feels heard, valued, and understood. Open communication serves as the foundation of trust, encompassing active listening, encouraging expression, and engaging in age-appropriate discussions.

> Access the download on components to open communication at www.meganmhamm.com/the-heart-of-the-matter.

Unconditional Acceptance: Unconditional acceptance is the cornerstone of building a healthy relationship. It involves respecting individuality, refraining judgement, and modeling the treatment you expect from others. Fostering and adopting children come with challenges, but at its core, it's a relationship built on accepting your child for who they are and respecting their individuality – their special sauce that makes them unique. This respect forms the fertile ground where trust, understanding, and love flourish. As parents, it's crucial to acknowledge and celebrate who your child is, separate from their behavior and experiences as a foster and adopted child. At this stage, you strive to understand their worldview and individual talents, fostering a powerful affirmation of their individuality. **This respect contributes to building self-esteem, confidence, and a strong sense of identity.**

As a parent, getting caught in the cycle of asking why is easy. *Why did they do that? Why did they say that?* There is a time and a place for exploring and understanding "why" but; it's not the focus, not when building the relationship. Instead, concentrate on how they navigate the world, make mistakes along the way, and how you can support them. Recognize that your behavior serves as a compass and model for them to mimic. Treat your child with kindness, listen to their opinions, and empathize with their feelings. This modeling extends beyond your relationship and influences how your child interacts with others. Valuable lessons about treating others with dignity and kindness are learned from you by your children.

Moment of Truth

Remember to step away from the book, get your pencil and paper or your digital notepad and answer the questions honestly and with the purpose of self-discovery.

- What improvement can you make with your shared moments between you and your child over the last 5 days?
- Were there more positive or challenging interactions? And why did you answer that way?
- What does unconditional acceptance mean to you?
- How do you handle mistakes made by your child?

Cassie and her husband have continued their "daughter dates," eagerly anticipating them as much as Isabelle. Their activities range from simple ice cream outings at the park to visits to the arcade. During a window-shopping trip on their last outing, Cassie discovered Isabelle's love for dinosaurs. Yes, dinosaurs – for a girl! Isabelle picked them up, named them, and enthusiastically shared details about what they ate. Cassie was surprised but realized she had never really explored Isabelle's true interests, having filled her room with pinks, purples, blues, and princesses. Cassie decided she would ask Isabelle and have her more involved in decisions about herself. Cassie began weekly family talks. These talks discuss what went well, what can be improved, and what can make the next week better. Isabelle's responses vary, from "I wish we could eat ice cream every night" to "I don't want you to yell in the morning when I get up." These conversations have been eye-opening for Cassie, who takes the time to write them down and intentionally addresses most of Isabelle's requests. Despite meltdown moments, Cassie has realized Isabelle looks forward to their weekly check-ins and daughter dates. Cassie chuckled at the memory of Isabelle having a meltdown moment and paused to ask about the time they were leaving for the park. It wasn't funny at that moment, but Cassie has learned to find humor in even the most unexpected circumstances.

Chapter 7

Growing Resilient Hearts

"She stood in the storm, and when the wind did not blow her away, she adjusted her sails"
— *Elizabeth Edwards*

What is the ultimate goal you have for your child? What is your deepest desire for improved behavior, quality family time, and academic success? In every parent's heart, there's a silent prayer for their child—not just to endure life's storms but to thrive in the midst of them. Foster and adoptive parents often find themselves navigating storms and grappling with experiences that are both traumatic and transformative. **Resilience is the gift you give to your child for their future.** At its core, it is the ability to bounce back from adversity. Children emerging from traumatic backgrounds view resilience as a muscle requiring continual nurturing.

Acknowledge that, despite your efforts, you can't shield your child from heartbreak. However, you strive to prevent them from being broken by it. It is crucial for you to instill resilience in your foster and adopted child, aiding them in overcoming traumatic pasts. Others may perceive your child as a victim, fragile, and broken. Still, they possess untapped reserves of resilience that you, as their parent must nurture. When envisioning instilling resilience in your child, I visualize a sports coach or trainer. Their role during practice is to build skills and teach potential scenarios where those skills can be displayed. The coach guides you through the game, encourages you to use the skills you learned, and motivates you to pivot or adjust as needed. As a parent, you are your child's resiliency coach. You are teaching and modeling skills that will help them to continue to show resilience in their everyday lives.

To help you get started, I have compiled a list of eight strategies to help you increase resilience in your child:

1. Be a safe place for them to express their feelings, fears, hopes, and dreams without concerns of getting in trouble.
2. Find ways to be intentional in making meaningful memories – times to just have fun and enjoy each other.
3. Help them embrace the growth mindset that they can learn and do tough things.
4. Discover times to celebrate even the small wins such as getting a good behavior report from school.

5. Show them how to use self-care and coping to regulate their emotions.
6. Name the feelings they have and validate that having feelings is normal, it's how we show them that can get us in trouble.
7. Have support from others such as other family and community members.
8. Get involved in the community through volunteering or attending community events.

> Visit www.meganmhamm.com/the-heart-of-the-matter to access the toolkit for building resilience in foster and adopted children.

Moment of Truth

Remember to step away from the book, get your pencil and paper or your digital notepad and answer the questions honestly and with the purpose of self-discovery.

- What has been effective in how you teach resilience to your child?

- What could be improved?

- What is one resilience strategy that you can implement within the next week?

When describing Isabelle, Cassie will tell you that she is the strongest and most resilient person she has ever met. Even when Isabelle's world unravels during meltdown moments, Cassie can observe her care and concern for others. She can have a meltdown at 3:15 pm and wants to cuddle by 4:00 pm. Cassie finds it confusing. Cassie is still puzzled by how a person can transition from saying, "I hate living with you," to "have a great day" within a 10-minute car ride to school. One thing Cassie has noticed is that the meltdown moments are changing. She is uncertain about the nature of the change or how to articulate it, and she certainly does not want to jinx it. Nevertheless, they are changing. Cassie is uncertain whether the change is due to her altering how she perceives the meltdown moments, the relationship with Isabelle becoming more connected and robust, or a combination of both. Regardless, the meltdown behaviors persist, in short duration, and the recovery and reset is becoming easier to navigate. Every bit of progress holds significance to them, no matter how small.

Chapter 8

Mastering Meltdown Moments:

Using the H.E.A.R.T. Framework to De-Escalate with Compassion

> *"Compassion is to look beyond your own pain, to see the pain of others."*
> *— Yasmin Mogahed*

As a parent, dealing with meltdown moments becomes a challenge – especially for foster and adoptive parents whose child has experienced trauma. Meltdown moments occur more frequently, last longer and leave everyone feeling tired and isolated. The more meltdown moments create less connection to your child. Mastering meltdown moments with compassion fosters a deeper connection with your child. It becomes less about being a compassionate parent and more about trying to defuse the next situation. As a foster and adoptive parent, you have experienced instances filled with emotional highs and lows. Like many parents in similar situations, you may feel unprepared and overwhelmed during emotional storms. Your child's meltdown moments, ranging from tears to anger, are expressions of their feelings and echoes of their past traumas. The key to navigating these emotional waters lies in acknowledging your personal struggles in being able to support your child. It requires you, as a parent, to look beyond the surface of these meltdown moments to the underlying causes.

Your child's episodes of anger may not be solely directed towards you but maybe a manifestation of their fear, confusion, and past pain. Recognizing this, you begin approaching these situations with a softer, more empathetic demeanor. During meltdown moments, your child may be unable to make rational decisions resulting in different ways of responding to a trigger.

Again, it's important to clarify that a compassionate approach is not about dismissing or overlooking inappropriate behavior. Instead, it's about responding to such behavior in a way that acknowledges how your child feels while guiding them towards alternative ways of expressing their feelings.

Let me introduce you to *Mastering Meltdown Moments*. Mastering Meltdown Moments – a unique concept and framework for adoptive and foster parents – to feel empowered to handle meltdown moments skillfully and masterfully.

Three key insights to Mastering Meltdown Moments are:

- Be the compassionate anchor,
- Experiences influence behavior,
- Relationships are important.

I want to introduce the H.E.A.R.T. Framework to De-Escalating Behaviors with a Compassionate Approach.

H – Help with Calmness

E – Engage with Empathy

A – Assess Triggers

R – Respectful Limits and Choices

T – Take Time to Reflect

H

Help with Calmness

Throughout the meltdown moment, the goal for you as a parent is to remain calm. Your calmness will help your child's calmness and be an anchor to whatever is going on with your child.

Remaining calm will help your child calm down. Sounds easy, right? Just kidding; sometimes you feel the need to match them during their meltdowns because you don't want them to "have the power." When that is the thought process, you will enter a power struggle with your child. It is impossible to help your child regulate if you are not regulated.

This is the time to be able to maintain your composure, ground yourself in the needs of the child, and remain calm during their personal storm.

E

Engage with Empathy

It is important to acknowledge your child's feelings and behaviors without judgment during a meltdown. In supporting your child through their meltdown, it is important to validate their feelings. Name the feeling your child may be experiencing and let them know that whatever the feeling is, it's okay to have.

This is a great time to verbalize and talk through what you are observing, not what you are assuming is the trigger. Being able to validate your child's feeling, tell them they are seen, and understood is the compassionate connection that you need during a meltdown. This also becomes the time to show your child that you understand their big feelings.

A

Assess Triggers

All the steps in the H.E.A.R.T. Framework are important but being able to assess the triggers can be pivotal in decreasing the likelihood of future meltdown moments. Meltdown moments are your child's way of communicating unmet needs.

Be ready to play detective. It is important to shift your thoughts about your child's meltdown moments from a behavior problem to an unmet need. Investigate the needs of your child by asking questions.

- What is going on with your child?
- What is my child communicating with me?
- What was the trigger?

Being able to answer these questions will help you choose how to respond to your child's meltdown moments.

R

Respectful Limits and Choices

With respectful limits and choices, you can establish boundaries while empowering your child with choices. Again, understanding a behavior is not justifying the behavior. At all times the safety of yourself, your child, others, and the environment is a priority. A compassionate approach does not mean you allow your child to do whatever they choose to do.

Establish boundaries for everyone's safety and offer choices that are empowering to your child. Allow your child the time to make one of the given choices. If you have given 3 minutes to choose another activity, then enforce the limit at the end of that time. Remain calm and be consistent with your words and actions.

Take Time to Reflect

After the meltdown moment has ended, it is time to rest and reflect on what happened. This is the important time for you to focus on your self-care and ensure that your emotional needs are being met after mastering the meltdown behavior.

Pat yourself on the back! You and your child have survived a meltdown moment. Now consider: What worked? What didn't work? Are there any triggers that can be avoided in the future? Any calm-down techniques that can be used in the future?

> Visit www.meganmhamm.com/the-heart-of-the-matter to learn more about ways and strategies to Mastering Meltdown Moments

Moment of Truth

Remember to step away from the book, get your pencil and paper or your digital notepad and answer the questions honestly and with the purpose of self-discovery.

- How are you approaching meltdown moments?
- What is one thing you can do differently to add a more compassionate approach?
- Of the steps above, which one are you currently doing well? And which one do you notice as an area for growth?

Chapter 9

The Journey to Mended Hearts

"The journey of a thousand miles starts with a single step."

— Lao Tau

Nearly a year has passed, and every day, Cassie and Isabelle aspire to be better partners in their relationship. Isabelle's journey unfolded from a stranger to a foster child and, finally, to an adopted child. With its long and winding road, the journey sometimes left Cassie contemplating giving up. There were moments when Isabelle felt the urge to leave. Despite the challenges, they committed to trying, even when it felt impossible. Acknowledging the relationship's imperfections and that meltdown moments still occur, Cassie occasionally expresses frustration. However, they've established a perfectly imperfect way of reset and recovery. Those familiar with Cassie and Isabelle's story marvel at its transformation over these months. Those who once advised Cassie to give up now seek advice on how she persevered. Cassie draws from her experiences and has also learned to empathize with Isabelle's trauma, genuinely interested in getting to know her.

Within every parent's heart lies a seed of hope—for their child's future and a yearning for a connection beyond the ordinary. Regardless of what else you take away from your reading, consider that the parent-child relationship is inseparable - mirroring the foundation of healing. Healing is a journey undertaken by families together. This sentiment resonates, particularly for parents navigating the intricate world of fostering and adoption, where each day presents its own set of challenges and victories.

The spirit of the journey isn't discovered in the destination but in the steps taken together—sometimes small and simple, other times bold and confident. Using the healing metaphor as a journey, you will explore the importance of walking this path with your child, even when meltdowns occur, shame shows up, and fear clouds the way forward. Compassionate parenting's essence lies in realizing that the scars of past trauma won't vanish. Still, they can become less defining by prioritizing the relationship with self and the relationship with child. Exploring these relationships is an act of love, commitment, and willingness to explore your personal emotions.

Stepping Outside the Book

I have discussed the healing journey and healing together, but what does that really mean? Healing together involves exploring experiences and expressing emotions as a family. These activities can be facilitated by a professional or done informally as a family. Specifically designed, these activities aim to support each other during the healing journey.

1. Schedule a weekly family healing hour where the family engages in healing activities such as mindfulness, yoga, art therapy, play therapy, and/or music therapy. It's a planned, weekly family time dedicated to activities that connects you and your child and opens communication.

2. Create a feelings jar or box where family members can deposit notes about their emotions. You and your child can get as creative as you want to be in creating the jar. This provides a non-verbal

way for everyone to express emotions and feel validated.

3. Establish a family support plan easily accessible to all members, possibly posted in a common area.

4. Develop a family healing map, also functioning as a vision board for the family. The family will collaborate to find words, pictures, sayings, etc., representing their goals and accomplishments. Each family member should have a role to play in creating it.

I hope you consider implementing one or all of the listed activities. Stepping outside your comfort zone is part of the process. Remember, it won't resemble a sit-com with a pivotal kum-ba-ya moment reshaping the family landscape. It's the accumulation of small moments. Even if your child doesn't participate this week, they're still welcome next week. Even if your child experiences a meltdown over color choices this week, they're still welcome next week. Consistency and open invitations convey that they belong, are valued, and are seen.

> Access the toolkit for
> Chapter 9's Stepping Outside the Book at
> www.meganmhamm.com/the-heart-of-the-matter

Letter from the Author

Dear Reader,

It's been my honor to explore this journey of self-discovery with you. I am excited to know that you made it to the end of this book. This isn't meant to be an exhaustive guide for parenting foster and adopted children. I consider my book's purpose fulfilled if you gained insight into one aspect of the journey that you choose to incorporate today. I urge the world to pause and consider someone else's journey – and lead with compassion for their experiences. Take advantage of the companion course, filled with resources and insights at no extra cost. This book doesn't guarantee that challenging moments won't occur or that you'll handle them perfectly. However, I guarantee that consistently implementing one technique or strategy will make a difference. No matter how small.

Visit the website: www.meganmhamm.com for more resources.

Megan

www.ingramcontent.com/pod-product-compliance
Lightning Source LLC
Chambersburg PA
CBHW020946090426
42736CB00010B/1287